The Little
Fun on a S

Cost conscious ideas for early years activities

Written by
Sam Goodman and Elaine Massey
Edited by Sally Featherstone

Illustrations by Kerry Ingham

The Little Book of Fun on a Shoestring
ISBN 1-905019-47-5 • 978-1-905019-47-5

First published in the UK, January 2006

'Little Books' is a trade mark of Featherstone Education Ltd

Published in the United Kingdom by
Featherstone Education Ltd
44 - 46 High Street
Husbands Bosworth
Leicestershire
LE17 6LP

Contents

Introduction

About the book

We all know how important a high quality environment is for inspiring play and learning in the early years. Making your setting an exhilarating and stimulating place isn't just about money. It's about innovation, attitude, surprise and value of children's work and play. This Little Book offers you some tips to achieving an environment to be proud of, and one which inspires children to be excited, independent learners. The book offers busy practitioners a range of realistic ideas that can be used as described, or can be developed to suit your own needs.

Money is of course a major issue in most settings, and practitioners have devised many ways of raising the money they need for the little extras that make a difference. Sequins, glitter, shiny paper, fabric and wood offcuts, bargains from Pound Shops, sale items, are all acquired from the money raised when staff make cakes or organise sales, fairs and sponsored events. A small amount of money to add to the budget for the setting can make a big difference to the environment and the range of activities offered.

And, of course early years practitioners are very good at asking, noticing, offering, scrounging, cajoling and even bribing their friends, families and local community into parting with unwanted items free or at bargain prices. Carpet samples, ends of rolls of fabric and wallpaper, old net or shower curtains, sheets, saris, kitchen utensils, unwanted toys, half empty cans of paint, paper offcuts, magazine, newspapers, junk mail, packaging, are just a few of the items practitioners collect.

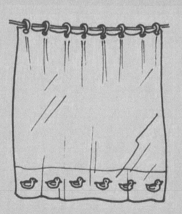

Practitioners are also generous in the additional work they do to raise funds - organising and entering for competitions, projects such as Artsmark, reviewing books for magazines, meeting with the Parents' Association or Management Committee to bid for funds, contacting local firms and charities for support. They never go shopping without an eye for a bargain, even their own children are not safe from the comment 'Do you still want this? I really need it for work'.

Parents, carers and families are also a frequent source of gifts and offers - paper, computer equipment, painting shirts, outgrown toys and outdoor play

equipment, hard hats, children's furniture, free pens and clipboards, ex-display items, and even a huge box of mixed screws, nails, bolts and washers are some examples of the offers parents have made through their workplaces or their contacts. The box of screws made a fabulous collage after weeks of being sorted, counted, arranged and made into patterns by the children.

Practitioners haunt places such as Wilkinson's, Ikea, Pound shops and local resource centres which offer items at extremely competitive prices, and have a vast range to stimulate your imagination.

Find your nearest resource centre or scrap store at (www.childrensscrapstore.co.uk). You will need to pay an annual fee which is adjusted to the size of your setting and the amount you intend to use the store. Then you can visit as often as you want and fill your trolley for less than £10 a time. Businesses donate their scrap - this can be anything: wood, material, ribbon, paper, card, wire, plastic cups, and many other more unusual items. Of course there is an element of chance when you visit - the resources you want may not be in stock, but that will only encourage you to be more inventive and adventurous - the children will surprise you with what they can do with unusual resources.

Share resources where possible, and always say 'YES' to offers. This can be done within your own organisation, with a local school, a playgroup or cluster group. It means there's an opportunity for everyone to have access to a wider range of resources.

Favourite items to supplement free or cheap resources

Here are some things you might like to add to your resources. Many of these can be on free access for children's own ideas as well as being used for specific projects planned by you.

- ✓ rice, lentils, dried beans and peas, nuts, seeds, conkers, leaves
- ✓ porridge oats, flour, cornflour, pasta
- ✓ sand, gravel, shiny pebbles, glass nuggets, beads
- ✓ paint of all sorts
- ✓ shaving foam, shaving gel
- ✓ small coloured trays, plastic bottles, shallow containers, boxes, bags, envelopes
- ✓ coloured papers, metallic and aluminium foil, foil containers
- ✓ lids and screw tops of different shapes and sizes
- ✓ glitter, sequins, beads, sequin waste, tinsel, decorations
- ✓ plastic sheeting, bubble wrap, corrugated card, cartons, boxes
- ✓ coloured PVC, cellophane, vinyl
- ✓ stickers, plain and printed
- ✓ safety mirrors including self adhesive mirror sheet
- ✓ magnets, magnetic sheet and strip
- ✓ ribbon, wool, gift boxes and bags, cosmetics boxes
- ✓ wrapping paper, festive string, tags, cards
- ✓ masking, parcel, double sided and sticky tape
- ✓ shreddings and packaging materials

Making the environment exciting for the children is easy to do. Alter the layout often, put toys on the floor that might usually be seen as table top toys, use your ceiling space for displays, don't ever be confined to boards for your displays, have different levels to work on - a different level can mean a different vision. Try the floor, under a table, in a tent, under an umbrella, behind a cupboard.

Don't be afraid to take risks. Sterile surroundings aren't what the children need. Don't be afraid to be guided by what YOU think is best for your children.

Equipment to borrow, share or buy

Every child needs to develop the confidence to use a digital camera, a printer, a CD player and other simple modern technology. Of course, younger or less experienced children may need more support and supervision until they gain confidence.

> **HEALTH & SAFETY**
> Make sure that gifts of electrical equipment are thoroughly tested by an accredited PAT engineer before you use them.

A CD player

- Not cheap, but vital for so many activities. Buy the best, most robust portable one you can afford. Get some advice about the best ones for children to use themselves and mark the buttons with stickers (green for play, red for stop) to make it easier for children to use.

A Digital Camera

- Digital cameras are now much cheaper, so take advice and look for bargains. Simple cameras, with neck or wrist straps are best for children to use independently. Make sure the camera downloads to your computer easily through a dock or simple memory stick, or add ...

A Digital Printer

- A simple desktop digital printer (such as an HP Photosmart) is easy for you and the children to use. Just insert the memory stick, look in the viewfinder for the photo you need and press PRINT for an instant record of activities. Such printers are now more affordable for everyone and if you haven't got a computer in your setting, you can have pictures instantly.

A word about Computers

- Computer packages are getting cheaper all the time, but they have still not reached the 'shoe-string' level. Ask around and you may get a used one as a gift (businesses can write off computers against tax if they give them to a good cause). Always have computers checked before use.

More equipment to borrow, share or buy

A Laminator

🔖 Access to a laminator is very useful. It's probably not worth buying if yours is a very small setting, but look for suitable organisations such as primary and secondary schools, libraries and local businesses where you might be allowed to use the laminator for the cost of the materials. Try laminating some more unusual things such as pressed flowers and leaves; or print your photos on regular paper and laminate them for a really professional look. Laminators get very hot and children get very excited by something new - so take care and don't ever let the children use it.

A Video Camera

🔖 Simple video cameras specially made for children are now available (sometimes at bargain prices). Look out for Digital Blue Cameras, specially made for easy use by children and very intuitive for adults too. This will give children another way to record their work and play.

A Shredder

🔖 You can now get desktop or personal shredders that may be more suitable and affordable for your setting. Look in office supply shops or bargain stores. This piece of equipment is almost essential if you want to make quick papier mache or home made paper, but shreddings have many other uses:

* fill an empty sand tray or cat litter tray with green shreddings and make a jungle for small world animals;
* shred blue paper for a sea scene;
* soak shredded paper and use it to mould scenery - mountains, volcanoes, seashores or moonscapes;
* try shredding cellophane or tissue for a change;
* fill a big container with shreddings for a new sort of 'find and guess' game;
* float shredded crepe paper in a full water tray and watch the water change colour;
* use wet shreddings to make drippy pictures.

> **HEALTH & SAFETY**
> Make sure that gifts of electrical equipment are thoroughly tested by an accredited PAT engineer before you use them.

Other useful stuff and some uses

Lids

* See how many different sorts of lids and tops you can collect:
    * tin lids from biscuit tins, paint cans, coffee tins etc
    * plastic lids from sandwich boxes, take away cartons, margarine tubs, tins of coffee, cottage cheese, ice cream
    * screw tops from washing liquid, fabric conditioner, deodourant, toothpaste tubes, peanut butter, cosmetics
    * plastic tops from aerosols of all sizes and types.
* Use them for:
    * printing, painting and collages
    * as disposable glue pots
    * for making small worlds on and in
    * as containers for small items such as sequins or beads.

Paint

HEALTH & SAFETY
Don't use gloss paint with children, and keep emulsion paint away from eyes and mouths. Offer disposable plastic gloves for extra protection.

* Decorator's emulsion paint is very useful for covering big surfaces. Ask parents to donate ends of cans or buy the cheapest branded buckets of white emulsion from a DIY store. Add some educational paint (liquid or powder) to colour it. Use the paint to:
    * cover big cardboard boxes that once held fridges or freezers to make houses, cars, trains, rockets. Use big brushes and diluted emulsion paint to cover them quickly. This will also make them shower-proof for use outside;
    * redecorate the inside of your home corner;
    * paint walls and fences semi-permanently to make a big drawing area that can be easily repainted;
    * cover windows for festive scenes; you can draw or make patterns in the paint, either before it dries or after (when you may need a plastic scraper to help);
    * paint sheets of newspaper to make a new surface for pictures, or as a cheap backing for a display.

Shaving foam

* Buy generic brands and choose the non-allergenic version to avoid skin reactions and strong perfumes. Use foam for finger painting, and colour it sometimes by putting a small blob of ready mixed paint on a corner of the table for the children to mix in.

Shaving gel

* Try shaving gel for a change of colour, texture and smell. Put it on a sheet of clear or coloured plastic, lining a builder's tray, indoors or on the ground outside.

Ribbon, wool and string

* Collect all sorts of ribbon, wool and string from:
    * presents, gifts and cosmetics
    * bargain bins in shops
    * market stalls
    * flower shops
    * after Christmas sales

and get children and families involved in collecting for you. Children love string and ribbon and will use it for many of their creations.

Wrapping paper, wallpaper, lining paper, card

* Ends of rolls of all sorts of papers can be requested from parents and friends or bought cheaply in sales and bargain bins. Children will respond well to having a good variety of papers and card to work with and choose from. Wrapping papers are good for making matching games, and for chidlren to cut and decorate cards, tags and parcels.

Photocopies

* and remember, prints of children's faces, names, eyes, hair, fingers and feet will intrigue others and make a most unusual addition to collage materials.

Relevant Development Statements and Early Learning Goals from the EYFS

Physical Development:

Use a range of small and large equipment

Handle tools and materials safely and with increasing control

Knowledge and Understanding of the World:

Find out about & identify the uses of everyday technology & use information & communication technology to support their learning

Build and construct with a range of objects

Investigate objects by using all of their senses

Creative Development:

Express and communicate their ideas, thoughts and feelings using a widening range of tools and materials

Work creatively on a small and large scale

Personal, Social and Emotional Development:

Be confident to try new activities, initiate ideas and speak in a familiar group

Work as part of a group or class, taking turns and sharing fairly

Continue to be interested, excited and motivated to learn

> **Note:** This book has been updated in line with the Early Years Foundation Stage (due for implementation in 2008). MD (Mathematical Development) has been replaced by PSRN (Problem Solving, Reasoning and Numeracy).

Problem Solving, Reasoning and Numeracy:

Show an interest in numbers and counting

Order items by length

Use everyday words to describe position

Count reliably up to 10 everyday objects

Communication, Language and Literacy:

Extend their vocabulary, exploring the meanings and sounds of new words

Interact with others, negotiating plans and activities and taking turns in conversations

11

Autumn on a Shoestring

Things to collect yourself, and to ask for from parents

- ❀ material, wool, string, ribbon, paper, tissue, sweet wrappers, crepe paper etc. in Autumnal colours (gold, yellow, red, orange, brown)
- ❀ try orange lentils, Borlotti beans or red kidney beans too
- ❀ leaves, twigs, cones, acorns, conkers
- ❀ a clear water tray, builder's tray or container to use as a trough
- ❀ PVA glue or wood glue
- ❀ bronze or gold spray
- ❀ card (cut up cardboard boxes and cartons), plastic containers

And for the walk:

- ❀ carrier bags
- ❀ suitable clothing and footwear, plus extra wellies for children who don't have their own

Autumn Walks

- Use your grounds, road, field (or even a neighbouring school's field) to go on an Autumn walk. Dress warmly and wear wellies.
- Take a few carrier bags. Collect whatever you find.
- MAKE TIME to play in the leaves. Throw them up in the air! If there are puddles .... splash in them!

When you get back

Create an Autumn trough

1. Use whatever is available for you to adapt. An old small clear water tray on a stand (or not!) is ideal. Maybe use a clear toy box.
2. The trough could be decorated with gold, orange, yellow or red cellophane inside, and the legs of the stand could be covered in Autumnal coloured fabric.
3. Get the children to bring in autumnal items for the trough.
4. Talk about change and what happens at this time of year. Describe how a leaf or conker feels. What colour is it? How does it smell? How many leaves can you count? Are they the same size? The same shape? Where did you find these things?

Weave an Autumn trellis

1. Attach a piece of discarded (or donated) trellis to two chairs to display it, or tie it to two rounders poles, or hang it up at children's level.
2. Help the children to weave or tie wool, strips of fabric, tissue, ribbon through it.
3. Add leaves, twigs, feathers by hanging them from strings, putting them in small plastic bags, or tying them in.

Make Autumn stories

1. Use the Autumn things you collected on your walk to make stories.
2. Put them on a table, on the floor, on a mat or on material over a stool.
3. Make picture stories with the leaves, seeds and other things you found. Create stories, you could use a cone as a character and an acorn as baby. Make twigs into a bridge, stones into a path.
4. Photograph children's picture stories, jot down what they say, then start again!

Make Conker trails

1. Spray gold or bronze paint over pieces of stiff card or board. When dry, arrange conkers in a pattern and stick them down with PVA glue or strong wood glue. Use lots of glue.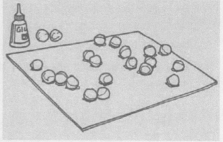
2. When dry, children can take their fingers walking to follow the pattern round the conkers in twists, spirals and lines.
3. Count the conkers. Use the sense of touch to explore.
4. These trails can be used indoors or outdoors. Lean them against a cupboard or tie them to a post at different child heights outside.

Make more trails

1. Make temporary trails on the floor with conkers. Can the children follow the trail with their feet or their fingers?
2. Try driving a toy car along the trail - or walking play people, compare bears, dinosaurs to follow the trail.
3. Where does the trail lead? Make surprise trails for the children and suggest they make them for each other.

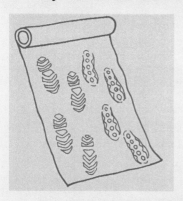

Make wellie prints

1. Look at the patterns on the soles of wellies and shoes. See how many different patterns there are. Look at different sizes - adult and children, babies and big brothers.
2. Make a collection of shoes and boots with different patterns for the children to try on. Put some paint in a shallow container and let the children step into paint and walk along paper.
3. Try ends of rolls of wallpaper. Most people have some of these. Explore the different patterns and sizes. Count and compare the prints.
4. Explore making muddy footprints on the path or play area - if there isn't any mud in your outdoor area, make your own with garden soil and water.

Make Autumn hangings

1. Using the items you have collected together, make pockets of Autumn colour and texture. Try leaves, seeds, nuts and berries, feathers, autumn flower petals, little stones
2. Plastic clear lids from food products are an ideal base, but you could use small plastic food trays or cut the sides of margarine and cottage cheese tubs down to make them into shallow trays.
3. Pour PVA glue to cover the whole lid, so the children can arrange the items in the glue as they want.
4. When they are dry you should be able to pop the hangings out of the plastic containers - the glue will dry clear, so the hangings can be displayed on strips of ribbon or coloured string. Hanging them in a window will enhance their effect.

Make Hanging Autumn collections

1. You need some clear, sticky backed plastic for this simple activity.
2. Cut pairs of squares, circles and rectangles of plastic (10cm/4" to 15cm/6" across).
3. Peel the backing from one sheet, place on a flat surface, and cover with a selection of your collected Autumn items.
4. When the children are happy with their creations, peel the matching sheet and help them to sandwich their collection (sticky sides together).
5. Either punch holes in or attach cotton to the collections for hanging in a window or for making a mobile.
   (flower petals and small leaves look particularly lovely!)

Development Statements and Early Learning Goals

PD: Manipulate materials to achieve a planned effect; Explore malleable materials; Engage in activities requiring hand- eye co-ordination.

K&U: Show an awareness of change; Notice & comment on patterns; Show an interest in the world in which they live.

CD: Pretend that one object represents another even when objects have characteristics in common; Experiment to create different textures; Respond in a variety of ways to what they see, hear, smell touch & feel; Understand different media can be combined.

PSED: Maintain attention & concentrate appropriately.

PSRN: Count reliably up to 10 objects; Match some shapes by recognising similarities and orientation.

CLLD: Build up vocabulary that reflects the breadth of their experiences; Talk activities through; Interact with others, negotiating plans & activities & taking turns in conversation.

15

Wet and Wild!

Things to collect yourself, and to ask for from parents

* all sorts and sizes of water trays and containers - trays, boxes, builder's trays, bowls etc (Pound shops are cheap sources)
* watertight bowls & boxes - fridge and sandwich boxes are ideal
* tools to catch things - tea strainers, sieves, tongs, fishing nets
* 'treasure' for the water - sequins, glitter flakes, beads, coloured stones
* hand whisks, cutlery
* brushes of all sorts and sizes, roller, buckets
* containers of all shapes & sizes, clear and coloured
* blackboards, clear tubing, concertina piping
* food colouring or ready mixed paint to colour the water
* oils & essences to add smells to non bubbly water
* washing up liquids with different smells

Check for any allergies before using perfumed oils or liquids.

Warning: This is a messy activity, make sure the children are well protected, but remember that some aprons can inhibit free movement.

Catch them!

1. Fill a large container or water tray with water and let the children help to add some 'treasure' - sequins, shiny stones, glass 'beads', glitter flakes.
2. Start by offering sieves to catch the treasure, and small containers for collections. As the children get used to the activity, offer smaller tools, such as tea strainers and then tongs for honing fine motor skills.
3. Try catching one colour only, or one sort of treasure.
4. Count how many objects you can catch. How many can you catch at once in a tea strainer? In a sieve?

Something/somewhere different

1. Put water trays and containers in different places, and at different heights. Try some of these:

   One container on a stand or table, one on the floor;
   One indoors and one outside;
   A very small container with very small tools, and a big one with very big tools;
   A very shallow, big container and a very deep one;
   One on a table and one underneath the same table;
   One on the grass, one on the path;
   Different containers with different coloured water.

2. Try to keep this variety going, it will keep the children engaged and thinking. And it doesn't cost anything to be imaginative.

Bubbles

1. Bubbly water is great fun. Washing up liquid with different fragrances can also offer a second dimension to this water play!
2. Let the children add the washing up liquid and whisk it up to create mountains of bubbles! Talk about how this happens and why.
3. Hide weighty objects (cutlery, toys) in the bottom of a bubbly tray. Can the children feel them? Can they use their hands to guess what is at the bottom of the tray?
4. Can the children catch the bubbles? Make ice creams in plastic cups?

Moving water

1. Suspend a piece of guttering between 2 water trays. Cup hooks and strong string are excellent for this purpose! Put coloured water in one tray, Movement between the trays will make what happen?
2. One end of the guttering suspended high will make the water move faster - how can we make the water move slowly? Use pulleys to alter height & angle of the guttering. See what happens.
3. Add a second piece of guttering.
4. Watch coloured water move along clear tubing.
5. Try using concertina tubing to see how the water is moving.

Contain that water!

1. Collect lots of different containers, and have selections which are coloured, and those that are clear.
2. Fabric conditioner bottles are now available in an enormous choice of colours, shapes and sizes.
3. Parents can collect some containers but look out for others at your local scrapstore.

What colour?

1. Coloured water is ideal for use in clear containers. Often water trays are themselves coloured and so use of that colour may not be seen to its fullest advantage. Powder paint, food colouring or even crepe paper left for a while in the water will add colour.

Watch out for skin allergies.

Do cover up! Use aprons and have spare clothes available too. Water is such fun and it's a shame to inhibit play because of getting wet.

Water painting

1. Give children buckets and brushes, so they can be decorators.
2. Offer huge decorators brushes as well as finer brushes and rollers etc.
3. Let them paint the shed, the playground or the wall. Anywhere water-proof, and when the water dries there will be a new canvas once more.

In the water ...

1. Use the water tray as an aid to counting. Make some fish from heavy duty plastic (cut thick plastic bags or cheap thin plastic place mats). Float them in the water tray and offer the children small nets and bowls for their catch.
2. Float plastic numbers or shapes for children to count.
3. Tie small magnets to the end of home made fishing rods (try cheap chopsticks and thin string). Slip a paper clip on your numbers or plastic fish and play magnetic fishing.
4. Practice colour recognition by challenging the children to catch fish of a particular colour.

And washing ...

1. Offer buckets and sponges to wash the outdoor and wheeled toys.
2. Hang a washing line outside, put a bowl of bubbly water nearby and wash the doll's clothes in the garden.
3. And how about a hose on a hot day?

Development Statements and Early Learning Goals

PD: Handle tools with increasing control; Use tools to affect changes to the materials

K&U: Investigate objects & materials by using appropriate senses; Ask why things happen & how things work.

CD: Respond in a variety of ways to what they see, smell, touch & feel; Play alongside other children who are engaged in the same theme.

PSED: Be confident to try new activities; Continue to be motivated to learn.

PSRN: Say & use number names in familiar contexts; Use everyday words to sescribe position.

CLL: Extend vocabulary, exploring meanings and sounds of new words; Interact with others, negotiating plans and activities and taking turns in conversation.

Budget Ideas for Display with a Difference

Use something different

👁 Displaying children's work is an important part of making a child feel their contributions are interesting and valued. To see something they have created displayed for all to notice gives an added sense of fulfilment to activities.

👁 Gone are the days of displaying on boards alone, and gone are the days when display was the wallpaper of the classroom or setting. Look for different spaces to present children's work, look for unusual ideas and materials, to surprise them and make them really look. See past the obvious uses for materials and resources, try new ways of using traditional materials.

👁 Involve the children in display - ask them what they think, how they would like to display their work. Give them their own places to display their work.

Or try some of these

- Rounders posts (or poles in bases).
- Set some broom handles in buckets of ready mixed concrete and use them to make signs, hang posters and pictures, make screens.
- Use strong cardboard tubes from the middle of carpet or fabric rolls standing in boxes filled with sand or gravel.
- Shower curtains are cheap surfaces to stick or paint on - they are also good for outdoor waterproof displays.
- Cut open some green plastic gardening bags.
- Hang up unwanted CD's in trees, bushes or from the ceiling.
- Hang things from ribbon strips, lengths of string, strips of plastic, wire coat hangers.
- Garden canes and green garden sticks make good supports for flags, figures or small pictures.
- Double sided tape is a neat cheap solution for difficult surfaces.
- Use garden trellis and netting, clothes lines and pegs, fabric remnants, Quadro tubes.
- Open out big cardboard boxes and paint them with emulsion paint to make pinboards.
- Hang beads, feathers, flowers, leaves on fishing line, strings or threads.

Make mobiles

- Use a piece of QUADRO pushed into a base (or a strong cardboard tube standing in a sand filled container).
- Thread through two short garden canes at different heights. The QUADRO already has holes in it but the tubing will need holes, made carefully with a sharp knife. Attach the canes securely with tape. At the end of each cane glue a bead (to protect children's eyes).
- Wrap coloured fabric or crepe paper around the whole shape of the mobile.
- Hang a strip of material from each arm, securing with staples. Display children's work or photographs on the strips. Gold netting is wonderful for festive pictures!

21

More mobiles

- Hang things from a wire coat hanger, or hang several coat hangers from each other for a bigger construction.
- Hang a branch in your setting or garden and decorate with natural objects or children's creations made from feathers, leaves, beads, wool.
- Find an old standard lamp in a charity shop (or ask parents) and use this to hang things from.

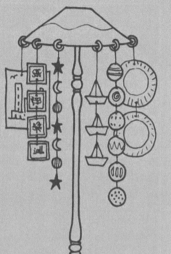

- Using a rounders post and base, make yourself a display post. Find a long cardboard tube, paint it, spray it or stick material on it. Help the children to attach pictures as they are completed. A simple, immediate and quickly changed display of work.
- Add pieces of wire to the post and attach work to the end of the wire. Santa faces, Chinese dragons, flowers or butterflies suspended on wire looked specially effective. The wires will wave gently in a draught as doors are opened, making the objects move.

Shower curtains

- Outdoor areas can be enhanced dramatically by bright colourful shower curtains, and these are now very cheap.
- Hang shower curtains from batons and hooks, indoors or outside.
- They are particularly useful outside because they are waterproof. Laminate pictures, photos, mark making, and attach them with strong double sided tape.
- You can also use shower curtains as dividers for areas - children could spray patterns on them using small garden sprays and a mixture of water and food colouring with a bit of PVA glue added.
- A blue curtain can be the sea, a green could be grass. Work with the children to add animals, fish, flowers, trees and people (adding some white glue to the paint will help it to stick.

Plastic bags

- Cut green garden rubbish bags to make vines and greenery for jungles, and tropical areas. Children can cut this too, as long as you have good scissors.

- Open the bag up and, using sharp scissors, cut into rough strips. Experiment with making snips and cuts and scoops in the plastic along the edges of the strips and then hang them up.

- This is perfect coverage for outdoors because it will be waterproof. If you have a covered outdoor area, attach strips overhead in a random way. Or hang them under climbing frames, in tunnels, from washing lines.

- Wrap them around pipes and wooden posts to complete the look, adding laminated flowers, insects, butterflies etc and you will have a new environment for play.

- AND - plastic bag strips are brilliant for outdoor weaving and tying through fences, bushes or garden netting.

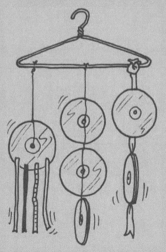

Compact Discs

- Unwanted CD's are a brilliant resource. Get parents collecting for you - many come free in magazines and in the post, and are unwanted gifts! Use double sided tape to attach them to a wall or fence to explore reflections and rainbow colours.

- Paint on them, use them for collage, use them as bases for clay or dough work. Stick them back to back with ribbon or string between them and they can be hung.

- Add three or four to a strip; add two or three strips to a garden cane, and you have a mobile!

Ribbon strips and banners

- Long pieces of ribbon can be used to display a variety of work, using the ribbon horizontally or vertically. Ribbon of about an inch wide is great

for displaying photographs. You can attach it to a hook anywhere in your setting, so you don't need more wall space for display.

- Banners are made simply by folding a piece of material over a garden cane, stapling the folded-over edge, and attaching loops of string to hang on hooks. Paintings look fabulous displayed in this way. Look out for unusual fabrics and netting (such as vegetable sacks).

Garden cane lines

- Looking for ways to use wasted space can lead to very inventive ideas. Look round your setting for odd corners, spaces between furniture, over or under windows, the backs of doors, windowsills, cloakrooms or corridors. You'll be surprised where you can put a display!

- Fix a vertical garden cane at each end of low cupboard units (use duct tape for firm fixing). Cover with paper or fabric, or paint the canes.

- Tie ribbon or string between the two to create a line. If the canes are tall you may be able to fit two lines in. Use them for numbers, for pictures or reminders for your current topic. Display photographs, letters, notices.

- Put items in plastic bags and hang them on the lines for talking about, counting or just looking at.

- Remember to involve the children wherever possible. For instance let them choose the colour ribbon to use, wrap the posts with fabric, hang or peg things on lines, put up their own work. If children help, try to resist 'titivating' their efforts - they will get more discerning with practice and the important thing is to give them ownership of their display as well as their work.

- Talk about the displays and use them for continuing learning.

Ship Ahoy - a Pirates' Tale

Things to collect yourself, and to ask for from parents

- stripey teeshirts
- old shorts
- leggings to cut short
- big hooped earrings or curtain rings on elastic
- scarves
- face paint for moustaches and scars
- toy telescopes - or make your own from cardboard tubes, covered in foil
- eye patches - made from black card threaded with elastic
- cardboard cutlasses
- batons or plastic hooks stuck to walls of the ceiling to suspend your rigging and masts

More things to collect, make or find

- pirate party bunting or flags
- an old box or plastic tub filled with beads, shiny buttons, plastic gems, old coins, tokens for your Treasure Chest
- garden canes for attaching to flags and sails
- plastic garden chain to attach to your anchor
- large cardboard boxes
- sheets, or large pieces of material.

Setting up the ship

1. If you haven't got room for a big ship in your setting, why not turn your units or cupboards around (so that you can still access the equipment) and make a huge ship that way? The back of your units can be the sides of the ship with the sea lashing around!
2. Use stiff card (cut up a big box or carton) to make the bow of the ship. Staple this to cupboards or use strong double sided tape.
3. Make rigging from old ropes and suspend them from the ceiling down to the units.
4. Attach material to garden canes and drape from the ceiling for sails. A blue or green sheet on the floor can be the sea.

Making a Treasure Island

1. No need to splash out on an expensive toy island. All you need is a large board and some helpers.
2. Collect cardboard tubes, boxes, lots of newspaper and you can make your own.
3. Make caves at each corner so the children can play from all angles.
4. Use boxes or screwed up newspaper to make different heights with hills and streams, coming down to the sea at the edges of the board.
5. Paste sheets of newspaper all over and drape them over the boxes, mountains and hills. Put several thicknesses of pasted newspaper over everything and smooth down gently. This method dries much more quickly than papier mache.
6. When dry, let the children paint it and add trees, boats, jungle, animals.
7. Varnish it, add real sand, place on a blue sheet and play!

Essential sailing accessories

☞ Make a ships wheel out of a small PE hoop. Make spokes from rolled up newspaper and then roll brown paper around the whole wheel (brown parcel tape is cheap and quick).

☞ Look in the January sales for a large plastic Christmas bell. Cover with pasted newspaper and spray it gold. Hang in your ship.

☞ To make an anchor use a wire coat hanger for the shape, and then wrap lots of newspaper tightly around it until you have the desired size. Finish with a few layers of smooth paper or tape. Paint when dry. Spray the plastic chain with gold spray and throw it overboard.

More ideas

☞ Make small maps. Stain some thick paper with tea, so it looks old. Draw maps and pictures of islands and ships. Tear the edges for added effect. Don't forget to mark where the treasure is hidden!

☞ Laminate some maps to use outdoors, hide treasure for the children to find using the map. Let children make maps for each other.

☞ Display a large map on a wall near the ship. Make your own or look out for pirate party tablecloths.

☞ Make up pirate names for each other, and collect other seafaring words such as Ship ahoy, Lower the anchor, Shiver me timbers.

☞ Get a plastic parrot!

☞ Have a ship outside on your climbing frame.

☞ Sing songs about the sea.

☞ Children can make their own rowing boats, ships, and rafts out of big cardboard boxes.

☞ Hide treasure (beads, old coins, glass nuggets, shiny buttons) in sand, gloop or coloured water.

and finally

🏴 Make a huge palm tree from a hat stand, standard lamp, carpet roll tube or other tall framework and add coconuts (taste a real one, but don't hang it in your tree!).

🏴 Make a pirates' Cafe with 'Pirate pop', 'Captain's Cookies', 'Sea biscuits', or 'Sand cakes'.

🏴 Give the children a lot of clay to make a big island in the middle of a water tray. Surround it with water and add trees, boats and people for small world play.

🏴 Make caves and bury treasure in sand, compost or turf. Prop turf up with bricks or offcuts of wood.

🏴 Make boats with plastic and paper, and race them across water trays and down guttering.

🏴 Look at books about boats, tell stories, dance sailor dances, sing sea shanties.

🏴 Make flags and bunting with triangles cut from old material, hang them on the climbing frame and see it fly in the wind.

🏴 Imagine what you can see through a telescope, what you might find on an island, what treasure really is.

Development Statements and Early Learning Goals

PD: Move with confidence, imagination and in safety; Use a range of small and large equipment; Handle tools, objects, construction materials with increasing control.

K&U: Build and construct with a wide range of objects.

CD: Use their imagination in imaginative and role play; Express and communicate their ideas, thoughts and feelings by using a wide range of materials, tools, role play & movement.

PSED: Work as part of a group taking turns and sharing; Be confident to try new activities and initiate ideas.

PSRN: Use everyday words to describe position; Say and use number names; Count reliably up to 10 objects.

CLLD: Use language to imagine and recreate roles; Interact with others; Extend vocabulary, exploring meaning of new words.

I See the Moon

Think big!

- push tables together to make a launch pad
- find some steps
- try a wooden or plastic step stool for steps into the rocket (make sure this equipment is safe and sturdy, and that the children know how to use it)

Now collect:

- large pieces of card, silver foil, shiny buttons
- builders hats and old wellies, sprayed silver
- playdough, clay, plasticine, Modroc
- cardboard tubes
- lentils, split peas, gravel
- beige or brown fabric
- space, moon, rocket pictures (download some of the fantastic FREE ones on the NASA website by putting NASA in Google)

Make a BIG rocket

1. Collect together some of the things that the children could use - boxes, furniture, steps etc. or you could just leave it to their creative minds. You could look at some pictures to get ideas, or read a story.

2. Talk with the children about how you could make a really big rocket or spaceship - one that several children could play in together. Listen carefully to the children's ideas. They may not be the same as yours, but, given the chance, children will improvise with the simplest things.

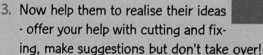

3. Now help them to realise their ideas - offer your help with cutting and fixing, make suggestions but don't take over!

4. Get them to mark where they want windows and doors, and help them with cutting (children will understand that an adult should do the knife bits). Offer foil and silver paint for the outside of the rocket. Take suggestions about the shape, size and organisation of the space.

5. Collect some shiny buttons, large sequins, shiny bottle tops and offer them for the children to make a control panel (or panels). Try plastic bottles stuck upside down on the control panel for lights. Offer coloured foils and cellophane for added effect.

Inside their rocket

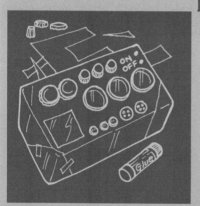

- Decorate the inside of the rocket with space pictures.
- Have mock windows with photographs or pictures of planets.
- Offer a couple of small stools to sit on.
- Use space wallpaper and borders, or space wrapping paper to add more colour for a themed experience.
- Talk about how to organise beds, food and drinks in a spaceship.

On and on, out into space

- Arrange photographs of planets around your setting. This will encourage language relating to your space or moon topic in areas outside the rocket.
- Find out as much information as possible. Help the children to use reference material such as books, video, DVD, and internet searches to find things out (put 'space' or 'moon' in Google to get lots of ideas).
- Use real names for the planets. Talk about what a star is, what is the sun? Which planet is furthest away? Which is nearest? The children will soon be able to talk with you about the red planet of Mars, about Venus, Jupiter, Pluto, Earth.

- Make a mobile from planets made from balloons covered with layers of pasted tissue or newspaper. Spray them and hang them from a coat hanger.

be an astronaut ...

- If you don't have an astronaut's outfit, or a simple white or silver suit, just spray wellies and a hard hat with silver paint.
- Cover shoe boxes with silver foil for air tanks, and fix them on with elastic.

On the surface of the moon:

- Arrange polystyrene shapes outside the rocket for craters and cover the floor with a beige or sandy brown sheet.
- Practice very slow moon walking.
- Have a Union Jack flag to plant on the Moon when you get there.
- Make sure you all know how to count down from ten to zero for take off.
- Make and laminate tickets to win a trip to the Moon or Mars.
- Make a moon buggy from boxes or from a trike with a box over it.
- Make individual rockets from cardboard rolls, foil and stickers.
- Use your sand tray as a space base for your rocket models. Try lentils, split peas or gravel instead of sand.

More ideas

- Make a moonscape from playdough, plasticine, clay, papier mache or Modroc, complete with craters for small world space play. Add rockets, space stations, shuttles, moon buggies, astronauts. If the space board is made from papier mache, set on a good strong board, it can be played with for a while and then packed away for future space topics!

- Suspend planets and stars over your base to add excitement to the imaginative play.

- Choose some suitable music for a space dance or adventure.

- Play the 'Doctor Who' music and travel in his time machine to other places and times. Let children record their own stories of their adventures, using a simple tape recorder.

- Use some percussion instruments to make some space music for dancing or acting out stories. Record the music so children can play it back in their own free play time.

- Use old mobile phones (with the batteries removed) as walkie talkies.

- Take photo sequences of the children's space stories to make books and displays.

Development Statements and Early Learning Goals

PD: Mount stairs or steps; Judge body space in relation to space available; Move with control and co ordination.

K&U: Show an interest in the world in which they live; Comment and ask questions about where they live and the natural world; Describe simple features of objects and events.

CD: Use available resources to create props to support role play; Play co operatively as part of a group to act out a narrative.

PSED: Dress and undress independently; Work as part of a group; Display high levels of involvement in activities.

PSRN: Use the language of size, such as greater and smaller; Use some number names accurately language in play.

CLL: Extend vocabulary; Use language to imagine and recreate roles; Interact with others.

Going on Holiday!

Things to collect yourself, and to ask for from parents:

- old, new and blank postcards
- a globe, maps, atlas
- a selection of luggage - holdalls, cases, rucksacks, small wheelie cases
- tents or sheets
- suitable fabric for sand and sea
- holiday brochures
- holiday photographs, digital camera
- old or unwanted cameras or camcorders
- world music
- a selection of boxes
- parasols, windbreaks, beach mats, sun loungers, deckchairs, towels, swimsuits, beach bags, sunglasses, suntan lotion bottles (empty)
- small world sea or rock pool creatures; sea shells

Ask around

- Try your local travel agent for brochures, leaflets and posters.
- Ask parents, colleagues, friends to collect tickets, labels and other travel items.
- Make a travel agent's office from a table. Add long cardboard tubes at each end, and attach a roof (you can use this as a beach cafe later!).
- Offer the children the materials to make their own tickets, passports (with digital photos) and boarding cards for trains, boats or planes.
- Provide telephones and a computer keyboard for booking holidays.

Pack and go

- Talk about different sorts of holidays, the weather, what to take and what to wear, where to stay and what they will do and see (be sensitive to the circumstances of the children, and don't assume that everyone goes on foreign holidays).
- Offer a selection of clothes so children can pack their suitcases or bags for the holiday they choose.
- Talk about what happens at airports, railway and bus stations. Let the children choose which sort of transport they will use, and vary the situations from day to day.
- For an airport there could be a departure lounge with a few chairs. The aeroplane can be a row of seats or boxes. Air crew outfits and in flight meals add a touch of realism, and you could provide small trays or lids from shoe boxes for airline meals.

- Bus and train stations offer different opportunities, with ticket offices, waiting rooms, seats with tables, different trolleys for food.
- Provide a variety of luggage. Talk about size, weight etc. How can the luggage be moved about?
- Make or borrow a trolley to help with baggage problems.
- Don't forget to write and send some postcards!

Go on a cruise

- Make a liner or cruise ship from big boxes. Make it as big as you can - outdoors if possible. Add a bridge for the captain or some sails made from old sheets to sail away to a holiday island or on a cruise.

- Make individual boats from smaller boxes with oars or paddles (plastic tennis rackets or table tennis bats). Set these on a fabric sea and let children imagine their own journeys.

- For a canal barge, use some boxes in a long line and add painted pots, pans and kettles from second hand shops or car boot sales (paint them with a mixture of paint and white glue).

Caravans and mobile homes

- Make a caravan from a washing machine box, or use a play house as a base, adding card wheels and perhaps a driving position at the front.

- Furnish the mobile home with children's furniture, and explore folding tables and beds. Don't forget curtains and things like water carriers.

- And of course you could explore tents and camping - use a pop-up tent or suspend a rope between two bushes, trees or hooks in walls. Drape a sheet over and weight the edges down with bricks to make a bigger shelter.

Sightseeing

- A digital camera is a good investment. Make sure it is robust and simple enough for the children to use unaided.
- Also ask around for unwanted or old cameras and camcorders for role play.
- Display the pictures in your setting or let children make their own group photo album.
- Make postcards and post them in your own post box.
- Collect postcards from the children's own trips and display them.
- Establish a special character (a teddy or soft toy) in your setting, who can accompany children home at the weekends and on holiday. Give them a diary or notebook for photos and other souvenirs of their stays.

Down to the beach

- Make a beach in your outdoor area with lots of sand and pebbles. Add water for rock pools and go paddling.

- Try a beach cafe with an umbrella and deck chairs. Mix cocktails with food colouring and water and add some cocktail umbrellas. Or have ice creams made from cones of card.

- Fill a paddling pool with water, add blue colouring and some plastic sea creatures. Go fishing with nets.

- Make the sand tray into a miniature beach.

- Spread your beach towels on the 'sand', put on your sunscreen and your hat and sunbathe.

and another idea ...

- ☼ Have an Italian, American, French day. Try the food, dress in different clothes, learn some simple language such as 'Ola', 'Bonjour', 'Have a good day!'

- ☼ Don't forget to talk about safety in the sun and near the water.

- ☼ Have a beach shop for ice lollies, ice creams, flags, sunscreen, hats, flip flops, buckets, spades, postcards and souvenirs.

Development Statements and Early Learning Goals

PD: Move with confidence, imagination and in safety.

K&U: Find out about and identify some features of living things; Show an interest in the world in which they live; Know how to operate simple equipment.

CD: Use their imagination in imaginative and role play; Play co operatively as part of a group; Express and communicate ideas.

PSED: Dress and undress independently; Understand that people have different needs, views, cultures and beliefs that need to be treated with respect.

CLL: Interact with others; Take turns in conversation; Enjoy listening to and using spoken language; Speak clearly with confidence; Use language to imagine and recreate roles.

Building on a Budget

Things to collect yourself, and to ask for from parents

 child sized hard hats

 wellies

 jackets or waistcoats (make these from knitted fabric which doesn't need hemming)

 children's wheelbarrows

 child sized tools - spades, shovels, rakes, and woodwork tools (hammers, screwdrivers, saws)

 cones, pulleys, buckets

 bricks, sand, stools, crates, roadwork signs, guttering, ladders, tents

 water, paintbrushes,

 rulers, tape measures, cup hooks

 a selection of props, tools and items for children to improvise with (old spoons, screws, keys and locks, offcuts of wood etc)

Painters and decorators

- Old dry paint cans or new ones from your local scrapstore will turn any child into a budding builder or decorator.
- Fill cans with water and provide a selection of brushes and rollers.
- Add colour charts (from DIY stores) and home makeover magazines.
- Offer small clip boards and pens for notes, plans and drawings.

Taking safe risks

- ✓ Let the children take some calculated risks:
  working on different levels is fun and helps develop vocabulary;
  using tools takes care and concentration;
  sturdy stools and short ladders will add excitement to play;
  real tools are less likely to cause accidents, as long as safe use is carefully explained and rules are established early.
- ✓ Large construction pieces make the building site fun.
- ✓ Include big cardboard boxes to build with, different lengths of plastic or cardboard tubing (which carpet has been wrapped around) to add a bigger dimension to the work.
- ✓ Use large plastic bricks or bricks made from shoe boxes filled with sand to build big walls and structures, inspiring the children to use all the available space.

Can you fix it?

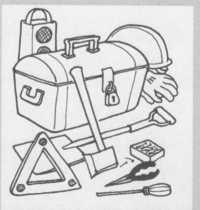

- Talk about what a builder does. Explore big jobs and small jobs.
- Take a walk to a building site near you. Invite different workmen in to show the children their skills (a carpenter; a painter; a bricklayer etc. Ask parents (both mums and dads) to come and show the children their DIY skills.
- Look at a selection of real, adult tools.

Reels and crates

Add some of these:

- Large empty cable reels to use as work surfaces or roll and stack round the site.

- Plastic crates for stacking or making into walls.

- Big tyres, rope and pulleys; buckets and other containers.

- Pulleys attached overhead or to a wall (cup hooks will work just as well with strong string).

- A selection of buckets and containers to use with the pulleys and fill with bricks, gravel and sand.

- Ramps, guttering and pipes to move objects and water into containers and wheelbarrows. Show children how to suspend these so that they can direct water, small balls or cotton reels into buckets, lorries or a home made cement mixer.

- A sturdy ramp resting on an old tractor tyre is ideal for pushing a wheelbarrow up to the top of a slope or pile of earth.

  Try your local scrapstore for these items.

- ☺ Children will need to think about how to move large and awkward shaped pieces of equipment. They will be challenged to work together and to give each other directions when moving around their busy site.

- ☺ They will also need to discuss ways of fixing things together, lifting heavy objects, moving items, balancing and attaching. They need plenty of time and opportunity to discuss, try things out and improve their ideas and techniques.

Making contacts

- Look up a local architect or builder, phone them (or get the children to) and ask if they have any plans you could borrow or have.
- Contact your local planning officer (at the council offices) and ask if they can help with plans or maps.
- Ask parents if they have plans or maps to lend for display or discussion.
- Use a computer to draw designs for houses and other buildings.
- Download some local maps or aerial photos and talk about plans and views.
- Talk about things like how water and electricity get into a house and where the bath water goes.

Have a look

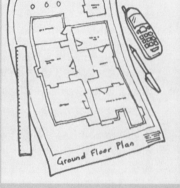

- Visit a building site and take some photos of what you see.
- Look on Amazon for videos of building, diggers at work and other construction footage.
- Contact manufacturers of building machinery or vehicles for catalogues and brochures, ask your local DIY stores for unwanted items, visit a builder's merchant to look at building materials.

Development Statements and Early Learning Goals

PD: Show an awareness of space, themselves and others; Handle tools, construction materials safely & with control; Use a range of small & large equipment; Move with confidence, imagination & in safety.

K&U: Build & construct with wide range of objects; Select tools & techniques to assemble & join materials.

CD: Use their imagination in imaginative role play; Play co-operatively as part of a group; Work creatively on a large or small scale; Express & communicate ideas & feelings.

PSED: Work as part of a group taking turns & sharing; Be confident to try new activities & initiate ideas.

PSRN: Use everyday words to describe position; Say & use number names in order in familiar contexts.

CLL: Interact with others; Take turns in conversation; Enjoy listening to and using spoken language; Speak clearly with confidence; Use language to imagine and recreate roles.

Let's Celebrate

Things to collect yourself, and to ask for from parents

* ✳ cheap wrapping paper or ends of rolls (ask parents)
* ✳ sellotape
* ✳ recycled or junk materials: a range of sizes of boxes, tins, cardboard tubes and other shapes to wrap
* ✳ card, or old greeting cards
* ✳ selection of ribbons and bows

and for the party:

* ✳ steering wheel or small PE hoop (for the bus)
* ✳ dressing up and party clothes - look for children's shirts, trousers, bridesmaids' dresses, bow ties etc in charity shops
* ✳ paper plates, tablecloths, plastic cutlery, napkins and balloons for the party
* ✳ toy food
* ✳ and maybe some real food for a real party

Parcels and packing

- ▪▪ Tell some stories about presents, birthdays and parties, presents, cards, packing, posting and delivering.
- ▪▪ Talk about what you need to pack and send parcels and cards, how parcels get to people, why things need to be wrapped up. Discuss addresses, stamps and packaging materials.
- ▪▪ Send a real parcel to the children at your setting, or visit your local Post Office. Try ordering something via the Internet, there are lots of sites where you can get free samples or catalogues.

Setting up for parcels and packing

- ✋ Set up a wrapping and packing station in your making area. Offer all sorts of wrapping papers, scissors, staplers, hole punches, ribbon, string, pens, envelopes, labels, stamps (see below for a good idea for making stamps!).
- ✋ Make some stamps. Get the children to draw some pictures for the stamps and scan them in (or use clip art). Use the computer to reduce the pictures. Copy and paste the pictures across and down the paper to make a sheet of stamps. Print these out and, if you want the real thing, sew lines between them with a sewing machine with no cotton in the needle. This will make perfect perforations! Or photocopy the sheet of stamps at the end of the book.
- ✋ Work with the children to make a post box, convert a wheeled toy into a post or delivery van or make an outdoor parcel office.

- ✋ Find some bags for the postmen and postwomen to carry on their bikes and some caps to wear. Offer some clip boards and pens for signatures.
- ✋ Suggest some suitable things for wrapping and discuss the difficulties of wrapping awkward shapes, fragile things and very big or small objects. Give plenty of scope for exploring wrapping, sticking, posting, addressing, stamping and delivering.

Choosing gifts and making cards

? Talk about choosing presents for people and for occasions. Make a gift shop in your setting, choose a range of gifts for different sorts, ages and types of people - babies, grandparents, brothers and sisters, mums and dads, aunts and uncles, friends.

? Collect some different sorts of cards as a stimulus for making their own. Don't forget other celebrations, such as Eid, Christmas, Divali, and other religious and cultural festivals, New Year, Anniversaries, New Baby etc.

? Make some gift tags for the presents, so everyone knows who they are to and from.

? Use catalogue pictures to make a matching game with people on one set and gifts on another. You could add a third element with cards or a range of samples of wrapping paper.

Planning parties and being a guest

✍ Offer some cards or postcards for writing invitations - add a list of all the children's names (and the adults too). Talk about house numbers, addresses, postcodes.

✍ What sort of party will it be? A wedding? A festival? A birthday? A Christening?

✍ Use the postbox or ask the post person to deliver invitations to the right people.

✍ Make lists of guests, gifts, things to buy or make for a party.

✍ Make party hats, place mats, table cloths, what to wear, games to play.

✍ Dress up. What sort of clothes would you wear?

✍ Decide how you will get to the party. Are the guests all going together in a bus or on a train? You could make a party bus from chairs with a hat and steering wheel for the driver. Make some tickets.

▌ And when you get there - what happens? You could play some party games (such as Pass the Parcel), sing songs and have a party meal with real or pretend food.

And another thing ...

- ✿ Have a Fancy Dress party, a barbecue, a Baby Party with all the dolls, a Pet Party with soft toys.
- ✿ Make some cakes, cheese straws, samosas, biscuits, jellies etc.
- ✿ Wrap some parcels and let the children guess what is inside.
- ✿ Turn your snack time into a party by hanging bunting, adding a party table cloth or napkins, singing party songs and having a guest of honour - a child or a puppet, soft toy or doll.
- ✿ Don't forget to take plenty of photos (or have a child photographer). Make sure you take photos of all the different activities - wrapping, posting, writing invitations, getting dressed up, going to and arriving at the party.

- ✿ When the children have had plenty of free play party activities, invite parents and families to a tea party in your setting. The children could make sandwiches and cakes, decorate your setting and be the hosts for the adults for a change.
- ✿ You don't really need an excuse to have a party or a picnic - or even a parade. Bring some music (or let the children bring favourite CDs) and sing, dance or play along with simple percussion instruments.

Development Statements and Early Learning Goals

PD: Handle tools, construction materials safely & with control; Use a range of small & large equipment; Move with confidence, imagination & in safety.

K&U: Select tools & techniques to join materials; Know how to operate simple equipment.

CD: Use imagination in music, dance and imaginative role play.

PSED: Work as part of a group; Dress & undress independently; Be confident to try new activities.

PSRN: Recognise numerals1-9; Count reliably up to 10 everyday objects; Match some shapes.

CLL: Interact with others taking turns in conversation; Attempt writing for different purposes.

In the Swim

Things to collect yourself, and to ask for from parents

- swimming goggles, masks, snorkels, flippers
- torches
- small world sea creatures.
- empty lemonade bottles for oxygen tanks
- large boxes or cartons to make a submarine
- inflatable sea creatures
- green bin liners or other plastic for seaweed
- blue rubble bags or blue, green or silver material for sea
- shower curtains
- sea shells and sand, lobster pots
- plastic bottles, garden canes, string, magnets
- underwater or sea music, sea songs such as Octopus Garden or Yellow Submarine
- white or black bin liners for huge suspended inflatable sea creatures

Make an underwater setting together

- Talk about what the children might need if they are going under the sea.
- Hang lots of sea shades of voile, netting or shower curtains from the ceiling.
- Add strips cut from green bin liners for seaweed.

- Children can create their own sea creatures with paint or collage, or try making 3D creatures out of inflated or paper stuffed bin bags decorated with fins, tails, sequins and beads. Make transparent sea creatures from plastic drinks bottles. Hang these from the ceiling.
- Make mermaids, seahorses and other sea creatures, and hide shiny sea jewels in the seaweed.
- Use a sand coloured sheet or a big shallow container of sand in part of the room for the seabed.

The Abyss!

- Try darkening a corner of your room by hanging up black fabrics or by moving some furniture. You could cover a pop up tent with a dark sheet to make it darker. Offer sequins and glitter for painting pictures of sea creatures to hang in the Abyss.
- Play underwater music and sounds.
- Put on diving gear, take a torch and 'swim' into the abyss to explore.

- Make a submarine from a huge box, a baby bath or an old water tray.

Miniatures

- Fill a water tray with water coloured blue or green. Add sequins and glitter and small world sea creatures (or fish cut from plastic) and provide small sieves for fishing. Add magnifying glasses to examine them.

Outside under the sea

🛁 Turn your outdoor area into an under the sea activity zone. Replicate an indoor scene, but use weatherproof materials such as bin liners or cheap shower curtains in ocean shades.

🛁 Again, hang plastic seaweed and laminated sea creatures painted by the children. Have a box filled with goggles, snorkels and flippers so the children can explore the sea.

🛁 Hide laminated pictures of sea creatures and challenge the divers to find matching pictures. How many mermaids can they find? Which crab is the odd one out? Find two matching fish.

One, two, three, four, five

〰️ Make fishing rods from garden canes, string and magnets.

〰️ Laminate a selection of sea creature pictures and clip a paper clip on each picture. Use blue plastic sheet, a plastic tablecloth, a paddling pool or a shower curtain for the sea. How many creatures can you catch?

〰️ Can you name them all?

Development Statements and Early Learning Goals

PD: Move with control & co-ordination; Handle tools safely & with increasing control.

K&U: Show an interest in the world they live in; Find out about some features of living things.

CD: Explore colour & texture; Use imagination in art & design, imaginative & role play; Begin to move to music.

PSED: Continue to be interested, excited & motivated to learn; Work as part of a group taking turns and sharing fairly.

PSRN: Count reliably; Use developing mathematical ideas.

CLLD: Manipulate objects with increasing control; Extend vocabulary; Use language to imagine & recreate roles.

In the Jungle

Things to collect yourself, and to ask for from parents

* green bin liners, green shower curtain or jungle fabric
* binoculars, cameras, backpacks, water bottles
* camouflaged clothing, netting, cellophane
* jungle animals (soft toys)
* jungle animals and jungle mat (small world play)
* pliable wire
* jungle wrapping paper, greeting cards
* large boxes (for cars and jeeps)
* plastic or polystyrene disposable plates
* rope, sleeping bags, sheets, pegs
* jungle music or jungle songs

In the jungle, the quiet jungle

🎧 Play jungle music with percussion instruments, sing jungle songs - try 'I went to visit the Jungle one Day, I saw a tiger along the way', or 'Mummy's taking us to the Jungle tomorrow.'

🎧 Tell jungle stories - Elmer, Rumble in the Jungle. Look at fact books about the jungle.

Make a waterproof jungle outside

✱ Snip and cut plastic vines and creepers from green garden sacks and hang these up from trees, washing lines, climbing apparatus or bushes.

✱ Add some snakes made from tights stuffed with old carrier bags.

✱ Hang coloured plastic flowers and big plastic leaves cut from carrier bags.

✱ A blue shower curtain hung up would make a great waterfall, a green one could cover a fence or wall.

✱ Fake grass would add realism to hard surfaces.

✱ Make animal faces from disposable plates painted with a mixture of paint and white glue. Hide the faces in the vines. Make monkey faces, with long concertina plastic bodies, arms and legs.

✱ Make some birds from feathers and string (or thin elastic). Hang them in the jungle.

✱ Play jungle music.

Make jungle games

➼ Jungle picture lotto - you need two pictures, exactly the same, for each animal. Buy cheap wrapping paper or greetings cards for your pictures, or use magazines, or pictures or clip art downloaded from the internet. Hide one set of animals outside in your jungle greenery and match them with the ones in your hand!

Make a rope bridge

* Let the children help to make a rope bridge on the floor, using card rectangles from cartons cut into strips and edged with a rope. Stick it down onto a roll of stair carpet (try asking parents for old carpet or use offcuts).

* Make the bridge narrow so it's tricky to walk along and take it over a blue fabric river.

* Make crocodiles for the river! Use egg boxes, folded-over card, triangular shaped or jagged polystyrene pieces for sharp teeth.

* Under the bridge at intervals, put large laminated pictures of crocodiles, snakes or hippos to add to the danger and excitement.

* Put large animal pictures in the grass.

* Add snakes around the bridge, and a few poisonous spiders too.

Mind the snakes!

☛ Fill lots of carrier bags and bin bags with crumpled newspaper and tie the tops with elastic bands.

☛ Put the bags all over the floor of the jungle and cover them with brown and green material.

☛ Place rubber snakes or ropes with snake faces, randomly in between. Can the children make their way through the jungle without treading on a snake? Can they walk on an uneven crunchy surface? Can they move without making a noise?

3D tabletop jungle

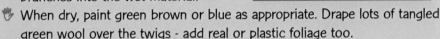

- Help the children to make a 3D jungle using a large board.
- Cover with lots of scrunched up sheets of newspaper.
- Cover this with flat sheets of pasted newspaper. Smooth some areas for rivers.
- Before it dries poke lots of twigs and branches into the wet material.
- When dry, paint green brown or blue as appropriate. Drape lots of tangled green wool over the twigs - add real or plastic foliage too.
- Leave a clearing to set up camp and make space for a rope bridge. Use play people and plastic jungle animals.

On safari

- Have a jungle dressing up box, inside or outside.
- Include animal masks, safari outfits, cameras, binoculars, water flasks, rucksacks, bug collecting boxes etc.
- Make a jeep out of a large box.
- Make a canoe out of a long box and take a trip down the river. Watch out for crocodiles and hippos! Make a camp with sheets for tents. Remember mosquito nets, sleeping bags and don't forget a fire (branches with red, yellow and orange cellophane underneath) to keep the wild animals away.
- Or have a jungle fancy dress day.

Development Statements and Early Learning Goals

PD: Move with confidence, imagination and in safety; Move with control & co-ordination; Travel over balancing equipment; Construct with large materials such as ccartons, fabric and planks; Mount steps using alternate feet.

K&U: Observe, find out about and identify features in the natural world; Build & construct with a wide range of objects.

CD: Explore colour, texture, shape and form in 2 and 3 dimensions; Recognise sounds; Match movements to music; Use their imagination in art, dance imaginative and role play.

PSED: Be confident to try new activities; Work as part of a group.

PSRN: Use everyday words to describe position; Use mathematical language in play.

CLL: Use language to imagine and recreate roles and experiences.

Light and Dark

Things to collect yourself, and to ask for from parents

* ✳ activity tunnels
* ✳ large barrels (clean)
* ✳ large pipes
* ✳ old sheets
* ✳ a selection of torches, battery operated lanterns
* ✳ large boxes
* ✳ night time play creatures (rabbits, moles, owls, foxes hedgehogs etc)
* ✳ luminous clothing/ luminous strips
* ✳ luminous stickers
* ✳ old CD's
* ✳ plastic mirrors or mirror sheet

What is dark and what is light?

? Talk about what light and dark mean. Discuss the moon, stars, night time and what we can see in the sky. When do we see stars?

? Talk about the sun, daytime and light. Discuss sunny days and cloudy days. Talk about times of day.

? Explain how all living things, animals, birds, insects, people need light and warmth from the sun.

? Talk about needing sleep and make a collection of nightwear!

Investigate tunnels

● Make and explore some tunnels, using play tunnels, fabrics and chairs, or cardboard tubes. Tunnel into sand. What is a tunnel for? Where can you find tunnels?

● Find out about and investigate animals that live underground. Why do they choose to live underground?

● Try to find some burrows or tunnels made by animals. How do we know where a mole has been? Talk about nocturnal homes where animals go to sleep.

Why do rabbits live underground?

● Find out who has travelled through a tunnel in a car, a train or a coach. What is it like in a tunnel?

Investigate caves

● Make caves indoors and outside. Use fabrics, cartons and boxes. Make caves under tables and behind cupboards. Hang ropes between two low points and make tunnels with dark fabrics.

● Join tunnels to caves. Explore them with torches and safe battery lanterns.

● Ask at your local scrap store for used, cleaned-out barrels. With the ends carefully cut off and sanded for safety, they make great tunnels and dark hidey holes which children can decorate as they wish. Put luminous, shiny and holographic stickers, mirrors or mobiles inside the tunnels. Explore with a torch and see if you can guess what is inside.

Let there be light

SAFETY GUIDANCE: If you light candles in your setting, you must make sure they are supervised at all times, and preferably securely fixed inside a jar or other flameproof container.

- Make a collection of candles to display. If you ask parents and friends they may have spare or partly used candles that you could have. Try charity and bargain shops for candles and candle holders. Tea lights are inexpensive and safer to use. Floating candles are effective and will be put out by the water if accidentally knocked!
- Talk about what candles are made from, what they feel like, what happens as they burn.
- Discuss where the children have seen candles (birthday cakes, church, at festivals or parties).
- Light a candle and talk about safety of matches and candles. Keep the candle at a safe distance.
- Watch the flame. Does it give much light?
- Talk about what it would have been like to live in a time when all lighting was like this.
- If you have a scented candle, smell the candle burning.

Investigate lights, lamps and torches

? Take a walk around your setting or your neighbourhood, and look at different lights and lamps. Don't forget desk lamps, lamps by mirrors, spotlights. Take some photos of the lamps you see.

? Use catalogues to make a picture collection of different sorts of lights and lamps. Remind children of the different sorts of lamps - bedside, work, security, decoration, fairy lights, shop windows, traffic, warning, and many more. Look at different lights, and talk about why we need lights.

? Children may have lamps or night lights in their bedrooms. Talk about what these are for.

? Look at torches. Investigate how torches work.

? Cover torches with coloured cellophane to make coloured lights.

Investigate light and vision

- How do people see at night? What helps them? What would happen if we had to find our way without any lights to help us?
- What happens in places where there are no lights at night - like the jungle, the desert, mountains or at sea?
- Try a day without using any lights in your setting - what is different? What is more difficult?
- How do animals see in the night? Which animals go out at night? Collect some information about these animals - is there anything you notice about them?

Investigate reflections

- Look at things that reflect light. Collect shiny objects and look at reflections in different things - spoons, saucepans, chrome objects, Christmas baubles, foil and reflective papers, metal tins, foil plates, and mirrors.
- Display safe mirrors and other shiny things. Try drawing your reflection in a mirror or shiny surfce.
- Collect a basket of shiny things - jewellery, decorations, foil shapes, chrome things, cutlery, ornaments. Put the basket on a piece of shiny material and offer some mirrors or mirror boxes to make reflections. Add shiny fabrics to dressing up boxes (wedding and evening wear and shiny shoes from charity shops or offered by families).
- Investigate kaleidoscopes, and try making one with a cardboard tube and some sequins or beads.
- Make a mobile from unwanted CDs, foil dishes, strips of foil and other free things that reflect colour and light. Hang the mobile indoors or outside where the wind will catch it. Add some tiny bells or shells.

and projections

- Borrow an overhead projector or a light table and explore transparent materials such as cellophane, clear plastic and tissue.
- Make a collection of everyday objects made from transparent and translucent materials. Try charity shops, car boot sales and supermarkets for coloured transparent picnic plates, glasses and cutlery.

There are lots more ideas in The Little Book of Light and Shadow.

Make a magical grotto

※ Ask around for unwanted fairy lights (or buy some cheaply in the Christmas sales!).

※ Decorate a dark corner of your setting with black sheets or other dark material.

※ Hang fairy lights and ropelight on your walls.

※ Add bead curtains, CDs, sequin fabric, to catch the light.

※ Offer torches and battey lanterns so children can shine them on the dark walls.

※ **MAKE SURE ALL LIGHTING IS SECURELY FIXED WITH NO TRAILING CABLES.**

Sit in your grotto and tell stories about night and day

- Hoot - Jane Hissey
- Whatever Next? - Jill Murphy
- Peace at Last - Jill Murphy
- Can't you Sleep Little Bear? - Martin Waddell
- Funny Bones- Janet and Alan Ahlberg
- Fly by Night - Juen Crebbin
- The Rescue Party - Nick Butterworth
- Hedgehog's Balloon- Nick Butterworth
- Wishing Moon- Lesley Harker
- It Was a Dark and Stormy Night - Alan Ahlberg
- Night Light - a Story for children afraid of the dark - Jack Dutro
- Night Monkey, Day Monkey - Julia Donaldson
- The Owl Who Was Afraid of the Dark - Jill Tomlinson (also available as an audio book)
- Mog in the Dark - Judith Kerr
- Dark, Dark, Tale - Ruth Brown
- Owl Babies - Martin Waddell
- Percy's Friend the Hedgehog - Nick Butterworth
- The Winter Hedgehog - Ann Cartwright
- Night Animals - Susan Meredith
- Nocturnal Animals and Classroom Nights (Science in Every Sense) Rhonda Vansant

Investigate shadows

- ☼ Go outside on a sunny day and explore shadows.
- ☼ Use chalk to draw round shadows of people and things.
- ☼ Make shadows indoors with an overhead projector and a big white sheet for a screen.
- ☼ Make shadow puppets from black painted card attached to garden sticks. Play your show on a screen.

and some more ideas ...

- ◆ Make a night time small world with cardboard tubes, branches, leaves and sticks for small world play with nocturnal animals and torches.
- ◆ Talk about people who work at night - police, nurses, ambulances, fire, shift workers, cinemas and theatres, caretakers, bin men, people who work in power stations, all night supermarkets and petrol stations, hospitals, airports etc.

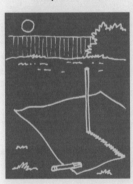

- ◆ Remember to celebrate festivals of light and fire - Chanukah, Divali, Candlemass, the Christmas story, Zhong Qiu (Chinese festival of the moon), Bonfire Night. Many Springtime festivals celebrate the return of the sun, light and warmth after the cold months of winter.
- ◆ Make a simple sundial from a stick and mark the place of the shadow each hour.
- ◆ Make a shadow shape Bingo game with black shadow pictures of everyday objects.

Development Statements and Early Learning Goals

PD: Travel through and under equipment; Move with confidence; Experiment with different ways of moving.

K&U: Investigate using all senses; Find out about features of living things; Ask questions about why things happen & how things work; Build & construct with range of objects; Begin to know about their own cultures & beliefs & those of others.

CD: Use their imagination in art & design, imaginative & role play & stories; Respond in a variety of ways to what they see, hear, touch & feel.

PSRN: Use everyday words to describe position.

CLL: Extend vocabulary, exploring new words; Sustain attentive listening, responding to what they have heard by relevant comments, questions or actions.

Use the Floor - it's free!

Things to collect yourself, and to ask for from parents so you can use your floor creatively

* large size 'junk' for modelling - really big boxes and cartons, long tubes, big bits of bubble wrap, boxes of packing wiggles, shreddings, wood shavings - and strong tape for sticking them together
* wool, straws. big sheets of paper, glitter, string etc
* chalk and big felt pens
* carpet samples, offcuts and mats (ask parents and local carpet shops)
* hoops and rope to demarcate spaces
* rolls of lining paper and wallpaper
* big shallow containers - builders' trays, plant trays, empty sand and water trays, baby baths, big plastic boxes
* big plastic or foam builidng bricks
* ribbon sticks and pieces of stretchy material for dance and movement

Use the floor instead

✳ Simply putting table top activities on the floor instead will bring a new slant to them - try some of these:

  ᛩ paint on big sheets or rolls of paper
  ᛩ construction toys in builders' trays or on carpet samples
  ᛩ modelling with recycled materials - build big and use the space
  ᛩ big bricks with low steps or stools so children can build high and wide
  ᛩ cushions and beanbags for stories and tapes
  ᛩ a picnic instead of a home corner
  ᛩ make a huge town or a long railway track by combining different sorts of construction and small world sets (a train track, a farm, a zoo, a town, an airport) join existing road mats into a new environment and try to keep the construction going over more than one day
  ᛩ chalk on a piece of dark carpet for a new sort of roadway.

Moving floor play

🅿 Offer a basket of ribbon sticks for dancing, or some big pieces of stretchy material for movement play. Add a CD player and some music.

🅿 Buy or make a small sized parachute for free parachute play by small groups of children.

🅿 Make a low stage or a mark out a curved area for performers and offer a basket of dressing up clothes, some props and a microphone (make one from a short tube with newspaper wrapped round the end to make it fatter - paint black and add a short piece of thick black wool or washing line).

🅿 Cut footprints from card or paper and tape them to the floor for a balancing or following game.

🅿 Put long ropes in wiggly lines on the floor for safe balancing challenges.

🅿 Put a box of simple percussion instruments in the middle of a hoop. Place small carpet samples

59

Floor level maths

🔑 Search out items for simple maths - sorting and counting - and offer these as floor level activities. Try some of these:

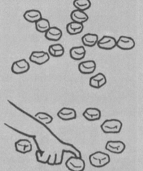

- ♀ Visit the January Sales for Christmas decorations - unbreakable baubles, strings of stars to cut into singles, tree decorations, tinsel, cones etc.
- ♀ Buy some cheap washing lines, dye them with food colouring or paint, cut them into lengths and tie these to make sorting circles.
- ♀ Buy cheap wrapping paper or sale rolls of wallpaper and let children cut them up to make matching sets of numbers, pictures, shapes or patterns. Old Christmas cards are fun <u>and</u> free!
- ♀ Collect junk mail and catalogues and use these for number and letter spotting with highlighters.
- ♀ Get some glass nuggets and some small placemats. Use these for non-permanent pattern making. Photograph the results.
- ♀ Collect empty plastic bottles with screw tops - get as many different sorts as you can and put them in a big container for a free game of Match the Top which is great for fine motor control.

A game or two on the floor

- ● Playing games on the floor will make you more inventive and the games more fun! Try some of these:

- ✋ Blow up a paddling pool for a magnetic fishing game.
- ✋ Sitting on your own carpet sample makes playing a simple game of Snap different.
- ✋ Spread out a set of matching cards for a Pairs game across a BIG space so children can walk between the cards to find the pairs.
- ✋ Offer children small, round, group-sized mats for games such as Pass the Parcel, Duck Duck Goose and other ring games in very small groups.

Under and through

- Make your furniture into playing space:
  - ♀ a rug over a table makes a great den;
  - ♀ an upside down table makes a boat or bus;
  - ♀ cupboards pushed together make a house;
  - ♀ a table on its side makes a puppet theatre, shop or vehicle;
  - ♀ a pop-up tent indoors makes a super room within a room for reading, resting or make believe;
  - ♀ the bottom shelf of a trolley or a shelf unit is a great place for play lying down;
  - ♀ a blanket over a few cushions makes a wonderful small world landscape.

Marking territory

☞ Children love being on the floor, but big groups of children sometimes find it difficult to manage the space when several groups are sharing it. Try these ideas:
  - ♦ lengths of rope tied and put down in circles;
  - ♦ carpet samples from sample books;
  - ♦ circles of thick knitted fabric or old blanket;
  - ♦ circles drawn in chalk (if you draw on fitted carpet, it comes off with a damp cloth!);
  - ♦ low walls built from big bricks;
  - ♦ a row of chairs or cushions;
  - ♦ masking tape is really good - it sticks to almost any surface and comes off without marking.

These ideas may help you to manage several different activities in the same space.

Development Statements and Early Learning Goals

PD: Move freely with pleasure and confidence; Use a range of small and large equipment; Use movement to express feelings.

K&U: Build and construct with a wide range of objects, selecting appropriate resources; Select tools and techniques to join materials they are using.

CD: Explore form in 2 or 3 dimensions; Express and communicate ideas through movement.

PSED: Work as part of a group; Show curiosity.

PSRN: Order items by length; Observe and use positional language; Explore pattern.

CLL Interact with others, negotiating plans and activities; Talk activities through reflecting on and modifying what they are doing.

Try Making Felt!

Making felt is a fascinating activity -
and a small bag of fleece goes a very long way!

What is felt?

Felt is made from wool fibres. Warmth and friction cause the overlapping scales on each fibre to open up and overlap and tangle with other scales. Warm water and friction bonds the fibres together and then you have felt!

What you need

* wool fibres, in a variety of colours (Merino wool is best, bought by weight, 1kg of mixed colours will last a long time) see end of book for suppliers
* sheets of bubble wrap approx A3 size (these can be used several times)
* pieces of net curtain about A4 size (these can also be re-used)
* bamboo mats or blinds (try bargain shops for mats and charity shops for blinds). Remove any strings or metal bits from blinds and cut them into metre lengths
* plastic bottle (milk or water bottles) with holes in the lids, filled with warm soapy water
* sequins, beads, ribbon, glitter

Preparation

As with any new activity, have a go yourself before embarking on the activity with your children.

Make the felt in the wet area or somewhere the floor can be mopped. The water that soaks the fibres initially, will be massaged out of the felt onto the table and the floor. Once all your equipment is gathered, preparation time is very short.

Starting off

1. Children can work in small groups or alone. Each child will want to make their own felt creation, but working alongside another child when at the massaging stage means there's someone to talk to or sing with while you rub!

2. Help the children to cut some short 'tufts' of wool fibres (approx 2cm in length) in colours they would like to use, and place ready, and then pull apart some long threads of other colours to make the background layers. It's important to do this before children's hands get wet and the wool sticks to them.

3. Put a piece of blind or a mat on the table, and a piece of net curtain on top (see photo).

4. The children can choose from the short pieces of wool, the colours they have chosen, spreading out the fibres with their fingers before placing them onto the net. The fibres they are putting down first will be the front or top of the felt, so they only need to be short in length.

   The pattern that they make at this stage, will be what is actually seen when the felt is dry.

5. The next layer will need pieces long enough to stretch vertically over the whole of the original work.

6. The third layer will also be of long fibres but, this time, placed in a horizontal direction. The children can work from one side, or turn the mat/blind for each layer they add.

7. Continue until at least three layers are completed. Some children may want to do more than three. More thin layers work better than fewer thick ones.

8. Now it's time to shake the warm soapy water all over the fibres, using a plastic bottle with holes punched in the top or a hand spray. Dilute washing up liquid works well. Use plenty of water.

9. Put another piece of net over the felt.

10. Help the children to roll the blind up, enclosing their work.

11. Now each child rolls the cylinder backwards and forwards on the table. This makes the friction needed to make the fibres turn into felt.

12. It takes some rolling to get the wool to bind together, but the children can take a look every five minutes by unrolling the parcel and turning the squares of netting one quarter turn each time.

13. When the fibres look very flat and stuck together, gently take the felt out and put it somewhere warm to dry.

14. The felt that the children make can be displayed in a variety of ways. Hang the pieces individually (pinned to boards covered with natural hessian, felt or calico) or join them to make a group piece of work.

Another way to do it

1. You can also make felt using a piece of bubble wrap. This is great fun!

2. Put a piece of bubble wrap on the table.

3. Work on the half nearest to you.

4. Follow instructions 1 to 9 above.

5. Now fold the top half of the bubble wrap over the soapy wet wool.

6. Show the children how to gently rub the parcel with their hands in a circular motion. This makes soapy bubbles.

7. Keep rubbing for at least 15 minutes, turning the parcel over every couple of minutes to rub both sides of the felt.

8. At this point the fibres should be starting to cling to each other as excess water is gradually squeezed out from between the pieces of bubble wrap. This part of the process is quite time consuming but most children enjoy it and will keep going.

9. There isn't a set amount of time to carry on the massaging process, but every now and then the children can open up the bubble wrap to see how the fibres are gradually changing into felt. Eventually the fibres will look very flat and bound together.

10. At this point the children can carefully peel their felt off the bubble wrap and place it somewhere flat to dry.

11. Dry away from direct heat, on paper towels or newspaper. The felt is usually ready the next day.

You can add threads or sequins to your work either during the process or afterwards!

Making a specific shape

❀ Once the children have mastered the process of making felt, it is easy to try making a specific shape.

❀ For instance, if you wanted to make flowers, put a simple outline of a flower under the bubble wrap before starting to lay out the fibres.

❀ Using thin strands of wet wool fibres trace over the outline of the flower (or other shape).

❀ Once the children have done this, the process is the same.

❀ Remember that to see the flower or outline shape you need to use a different colour of wool fibre for the next layer.

Or make a felt box or bowl

If you make a shape such as a flower, rather than drying it flat, dry it over a small container and spray it with starch. The felt should hold the shape it dries in.

Development Statements and Early Learning Goals

PD: Use simple tools to effect changes to the materials; Manipulate materials to achieve a planned effect.

K&U: Show an awareness of change; Ask questions about why things happen and how they work.

CD: Choose particular colours to use for a purpose; Talk about personal intentions, describing what they were trying to do.

PSED: Persist for extended periods of time at an activity of their choosing.

PSRN: Show interest by talking about shapes or arrangements; Use positional language.

CLL: Sustain attentive listening, responding to what they have heard by relevant comments, questions or actions; Build vocabulary that reflects the breadth of their experiences.

Make Paper!

What is papier mache?

Papier mache is a French term meaning literally 'chewed paper'. It is made from strips of pasted paper or paper pulp. You can make your own paper with the children using the same method.

What you need

- paper to recycle - the best sorts are absorbent types such as computer paper, typing paper, tissue paper, newsprint (the sort sold for painting), lining paper. Newspaper is suitable, but the printing ink will make your home made paper grey rather than white. Magazine paper is not very suitable, it's too shiny.
- paper shredder (optional) - table top shredders are available at bargain prices
- a watertight container (such as a big bowl or bucket) for soaking shredded paper
- a liquidiser or blender
- a bowl to hold the paper pulp
- a water tray (or large new cat litter tray)
- lots of newspapers to soak up excess water
- drying frame and netting (see opposite for ideas)
- boards for drying paper (see opposite for ideas)
- PVA glue to help hold the fibres together
- liquid starch to help size the paper (making it hold together)
- food colouring, coffee, tea, to colour your paper
- dried or small flowers, petals, glitter, potpourri, grass, feathers for added texture
- for scented paper, add aromatherapy oils, herbs, spices

Some help with equipment

Paper catching frames

You will need something to strain the paper pulp, and there are several sorts of things you could use - easiest first!

This sort can be used as it is!

* a splatter guard - a kitchen implement like a ping-pong bat with metal mesh that stops fat or water splattering from pans. Try bargain shops for these.

You can slide these frames into the leg of a pair of tights which can then be removed easily for drying:

* a piece of cane bent into a circle and tied, with net across;
* a wire coat hanger shaped into a circle, then pushed into the leg of a pair of tights; cut the leg off the tights and fix with an elastic band;
* the head of a fishing net slipped into the leg of a pair of tights.

These frames will need detachable pieces of netting

* an embroidery frame from a craft or hobby shop (it consists of two wooden hoops; which screw together and hold some net - possibly net curtain - between them);
* a small picture frame (any shape) with net curtain stretched across it and held in place by drawing pins.

Netting for catching the paper pulp

You can use any of the following:

* old net curtains; clean tights; fine plastic mesh

Drying and pressing boards

These boards need to be smooth, flat, waterproof and strong enough to stand on - try some of these bargain options:

* rectangular table mats (ask parents or grandparents, or try charity shops);
* thin plastic tablemats - sold in packs in some big supermarkets, these are ideal; strengthen them by putting a board on top when you stand on them;
* plastic chopping boards - these are cheap, indestructible and often come in packs;
* small squares of hardboard or plywood painted with gloss paint.

Getting ready

1. Use the shredder to shred the paper (children can help as long as they are carefully supervised). Children love the noise and the effect that the shredder has on the paper. Different shredders, also shred the paper in different ways.

2. If you are patient, or have no shredder, you can tear the paper into small pieces rather than shredding it. This takes longer, but it's a very good exercise for small hands and fingers.

3. When you have filled a big container with paper shreddings or paper bits, mix them with warm water. Let the children squeeze and squash the paper so it is all very wet.

4. Soak the mixture overnight. If you are in a hurry, you can speed the process up by pouring boiling water over the paper instead of warm water.

Be careful If children are near, they should stand well back from hot water, and of course, they must not put their hands in the mixture till it is cold right through. Remember, the mixture will retain heat in the middle!

When the mixture has soaked

5. Help the children to give it a good squeezing to make sure it is mixed. Talk about how it feels, and encourage the children to use descriptive words.

6. Set up the blender or liquidiser. Talk to the children about safety, and make sure an adult is present at all times.

7. Add about two thirds water to one third paper (about a handful).

8. Start the liquidiser, and give several medium length bursts. This should be enough to mix the paper to a pulp. If the machine appears to be struggling, add more water or try less paper.

9. Your paper mixture should look in a mushier (pulpy) state.

10. Tip this into a new bowl or bucket and repeat the process till you have pulped all the paper. This may take some time!

11. Add any colourings or oils at this stage. Other objects can be added later.

The very wet bit!

12. Fill a water tray (or other large shallow tray) about two thirds full with warm water (this is more comfortable for children's hands). The water has to be deep enough to immerse the frame, embroidery hoop, or other catcher you have devised.

13. Add a big blob of PVA glue and a capful of liquid starch to size the paper. It will make it stick together and provide a smoother surface.

14. Add five or six handfuls of pulp to the tray.

15. Use your hand to disperse the mixture and to see how thick it looks. If it looks and feels very watery, add more pulp. It isn't an exact science, but with practice you will know what is just the right amount to use.

16. You can also add spices, glitter thread, glitter, powdered paint, seeds, sequins, small beads, little flowers or petals and other items at this point. Don't add too many things or the paper pulp won't hold together

17. Stir again.

Go fishing - this bit is messy too!

18. Put some folded towels or a thick stack of newspaper on the floor by the bowl or tray.

19. Swish the paper and water mixture round, then put your 'net' in the tray while the water is still moving.

20. Hold the 'net' at the bottom of the mixture for a few seconds - the children could count to 20!

21. Slowly lift the net up through the water, keeping it flat. There should be pulp all over the surface of the net. If there are gaps, remove the net, add some more pulp to the water, stir the mixture and try again.

22. Holding it flat, put the net of pulp on the towels or newspapers, pulp side up.

And finally ...

23. Put a drying board shiny side down on top of the pulp.

24. Stand on the board - or let the children stand on their own. This should squeeze out all the water from the paper pulp. The heavier the weight and the longer you stand, the thinner and drier the paper will be.

25. The paper you have made will stick to the underneath of the board.

26. Leave to dry somewhere warm, but not too warm or it will buckle.

27. You now have paper!

And another thing ...

There are lots of different variations on this paper making theme. When you have been through the process once, be more adventurous and experiment!

* Make your paper different colours using food colouring or paint.
* Trap leaves and seeds by adding them at step 13.
* Add spices, scents and herbs - cinnamon, turmeric, tea leaves, dried thyme, lavender; or peppermint, rose or vanilla essence; or add aromatherapy oils.
* Add grass, leaves, flowers, seeds and petals.
* Try glitter, sequins, glitter string, gold thread.
* Adding torn crepe paper will dye the pulp - try red, green or purple.
* Add shiny bits of foil, lametta, tinsel, tiny stars or other little shaped sequins.

* Make very thin paper by pulping tissue paper into very small pieces and making the pulp very watery so the paper comes out thinner.
* Try using torn egg cartons, newspapers, cereal boxes, coloured ads from papers, maps and plans.

Using the paper

Here are some ideas to start you off:

* Display your paper with some photos taken during the process.
* Make photo frames by simply sticking a photo in the middle of a piece of paper (the rough edges will enhance it). Stick a piece of card to the back to stiffen it, or mount it in a picture frame.

* Make greeting cards by drawing straight onto the paper with felt pens, or by mounting children's pictures on the front of a folded piece of your paper.

You could make special pink paper for Valentines or Mothers' Day, yellow for spring, or red for Christmas.

* Use the paper for collage work, adding fabrics, beads, ribbon, sequins etc.
* Cut shapes from the paper to make gift tags or a mobile.

Development Statements and Early Learning Goals

PD: Use a range of small and large equipment; Explore materials; Use tools to effect changes to materials.

K&U: Show an awareness of change; Use simple techniques competently and appropriately; Talk about what is seen and happening.

CD: Experiment to create different textures.

PSED: Show curiosity; Persist for extended periods of time at an activity of their choosing.

PSRN: Use shapes appropriately for tasks.

CLL: Extend vocabulary exploring the meaning of new words.

We Love it!

On these pages you will find some uses for the top 'must-have' favourites of the authors.

Double sided tape

💜 Buy double sided tape in bulk... you'll need plenty! Use it for instant displays, indoors and outside. It sticks beautifully to shower curtains. For imaginative play when you haven't got days to wait for glue to dry on your boat, rocket or car, it is ideal.   Children can also stick it down on paper or material and sprinkle with glitter, rice, sequins, lentils, flower petals, seeds.

Shower curtains

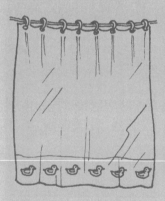

💜 Keep these on your shopping list. Shower curtains are cheap, bright and versatile. Use them for cutting up or covering display areas, especially outside, as they are weatherproof. Use for defining areas, for covering tables, and as play mats (children can use permanent markers on them and make their own play mats). Use with double sided tape to make instant dressing up clothes. Let the children use the curtains to make their own shelters.

Trays

💜 Particularly useful when working with small objects, as they contain the rice, split peas, porridge and limit the spillage. They also come in interesting shapes and differing sizes. Cover them to create a different work surface too. Use metal trays for magnetic games and letters. Use plant saucers and windowsill trays for individual sand and dough exploration. Use plant trays for draining water play equipment. Offer trays for children to carry equipment outside, it will help balance and coordination. Cover them with thin foam for noisy activities such as Lego and bead threading.

Pegs and clips

💜 Pegs are indispensable - get a range (plastic, wood, dolly pegs, bulldog clips, big, small and tiny). Make sure they are available for children to use too. Use them for quick tents and dens, instant displays, alterations to dressing up clothes, pegging shapes and or numbers onto number lines and trellis. Try a Treasure Hunt, pegging things around the setting and also onto plants and trees outside. Use as a fine motor tool for children to pick things up or to pluck clay from a big lump that you have hidden small objects in. Pegs are indispensable to pair up shoes and gloves and to hold wet paintings and other creative work.

Fabrics

💜 Collect as many different pieces of fabric as possible. Keep a wide selection in the dressing up box for fastening robes, gowns and capes. Have larger pieces available for tents and dens. Have blues for sea, sand colours for beach and moon play, and green for enhancing your small world play.

Fabrics on canes can make beautiful display back drops. Choose light voiles and chiffons to define areas, while ensuring supervision. Collect pieces of shiny fabrics, patterns, animal prints, flowers and pictures, fur, felt, lace, velvet, fake grass. Cheap plain material is good for printing or painting on. Cover a table top, box or stool with material and a make a different place to work or play.

Stools

💜 Stools can be used for a wide variety of purposes. A sturdy wooden stool can add an extra dimension to role play - the steps to reach shoes in the shoe shop, the steps up into the rocket or caravan. They can also add a dimension to building - 'Look how high these pieces of construction are now.' Low plastic step stools can be used as seating around a low table, they can be a bridge, a plank to walk from the pirate ship, and again used to reach higher when playing indoors and outside.

Battens and cup hooks

♥ Another key to a stimulating setting - get inspired with simple bits of wood, no drilling needed! Try to find various lengths of wood (possibly at a scrapstore), screw cup hooks (any sizes) into them and then attach them to furniture, walls, even the ceiling, using glue such as hard as nails. Make your displays more imaginative by hanging garden canes from them, suspending work on banners, displaying work across a corner. Zigzag invisible thread across from one baton to another. Hang beaded and ribbon curtains to create dividers; hang photographs. Use them to suspend fairy lights and rope lights. Rig up simple string pulleys.

Garden canes

♥ These are inexpensive and so versatile! Make a number line by attaching a cane to either end of your drawer or tray units, or to a low cupboard. Cover canes with crepe or ribbon before attaching them. Then secure ribbon from one cane to another to make your number or shape line, or to display work. Hang fabric from canes to make a divider. Masts for sails on your boat can be made with the help of canes.

Use them for a quick bus stop or street sign attached to a chair or table leg. Make a tepee from 3 or 4 canes secured together with string, ribbon or tape and you have a frame, which can you can use for display - filling it with wire and beads, wool, weaving, suspended treasures, findings from a walk. Use canes to make a hideout, or even for growing beans.

'Hard as Nails' glue

♥ This is quite simply a life saver. It dries quickly, and can take a heavy amount of weight. It is also easy to use, either from the gun or simply from a tube. It means no screwing into walls or ceilings , no wall plugs, and, more important, no mess!

1p	1p	1p	1p	1p
2p	2p	2p	2p	2p
5p	5p	5p	5p	5p
4p	4p	4p	4p	4p
10p	10p	10p	10p	10p
6p	6p	6p	6p	6p
3p	3p	3p	3p	3p
4p	4p	4p	4p	4p

Felt Making

For a fantastic range of wools and fleeces, felt making kits and lots of other wool related goodies try:

> Texere Yarns
> College Mill
> Barkerend Road
> Bradford
> West Yorkshire
> BD1 4AYU
> 01274 722191
> info@texere.co.uk

Scrapstores

To find your nearest Scrapstore:

> www.childrensscrapstore.co.uk

Notes, ideas and further contacts

If you have found this book useful you might also like ...

The Little Book of Outdoor Play
LB3
ISBN 1-902233-74-3

The Little Book of Science through Art
LB1
ISBN 1-902233-61-1

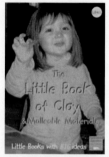

Clay & Malleable Materials
LB41
ISBN 1-905019-26-2

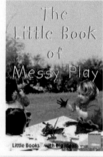

The Little Book of Messy Play
LB13
ISBN 1-904187-09-9

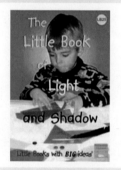

The Little Book of Light and Shadow
LB 25
ISBN 1-904187-81-1

The Little Book of Puppet Making
LB23
ISBN 1-904187-73-0

The Little Book of Bricks & Boxes
LB18
ISBN 1-904187-58-7

All available from

Featherstone Education

PO Box 6350

Lutterworth LE17 6ZA

T:0185 888 1212   F:0185 888 1360

on our web site

www.featherstone.uk.com

and from selected
book suppliers